Hold on
to the Mat

by Sue Graves and Maarten Lenoir

W
FRANKLIN WATTS
LONDON•SYDNEY

Jack and Mish
went to the fair
with Mum.

"Can I go on the slide?"
said Jack.

"Can I go on the slide, too?"
said Mish.

Jack and Mish
went up the slide.

"Sit on the mat,"
said Mum.

Mish sat on the mat.

"Hold on to the mat,"
said Mum.

Mish went down the slide.

She held on to the mat.

"Hold on to the mat,"
said Mum.

But Jack did not
hold on to the mat.
Jack let go.

Jack went up.

The mat went up.

"Oh no!"

shouted Mum.

Jack went down.

The mat went down.

"Oh no!"
shouted Mum.

Mum and Mish
looked at Jack.

"Can I go on the slide again?"
said Jack.

Story trail

Start at the beginning of the story trail. Ask your child to retell the story in their own words, pointing to each picture in turn to recall the sequence of events.

Start

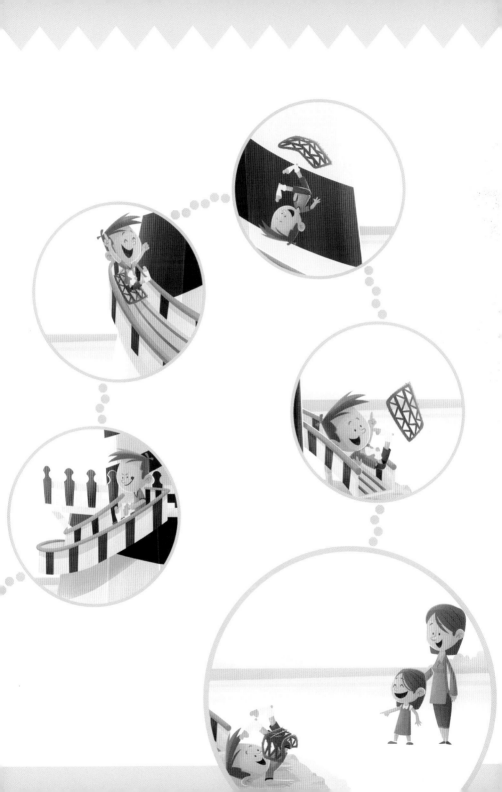

Independent Reading

This series is designed to provide an opportunity for your child to read on their own. These notes are written for you to help your child choose a book and to read it independently.

In school, your child's teacher will often be using reading books which have been banded to support the process of learning to read. Use the book band colour your child is reading in school to help you make a good choice. *Hold on to the Mat* is a good choice for children reading at Yellow Band in their classroom to read independently.

The aim of independent reading is to read this book with ease, so that your child enjoys the story and relates it to their own experiences.

About the book
Jack and Mish are at the fair with Mum. They both want to go on the helter-skelter slide. Mum tells them not to forget to hold on to the mat. Mish remembers, but Jack is having far too much fun.

Before reading
Help your child to learn how to make good choices by asking: "Why did you choose this book? Why do you think you will enjoy it?" Look at the cover together and ask: "What do you think the story will be about?" Support your child to think of what they already know about the story context. Read the title aloud and ask: "Where do you think the children are? What will the mat be used for?" Remind your child that they can try to sound out the letters to make a word if they get stuck.

Decide together whether your child will read the story independently or read it aloud to you. When books are short, as at Yellow Band, your child may wish to do both!

During reading

If reading aloud, support your child if they hesitate or ask for help by telling the word. Remind your child of what they know and what they can do independently.

If reading to themselves, remind your child that they can come and ask for your help if stuck.

After reading

Support comprehension by asking your child to tell you about the story. Help your child think about the messages in the book that go beyond the story and ask: "Do you think that Jack is good at doing as he's told? Why/why not?"

Give your child a chance to respond to the story: "Did you have a favourite part? Which ride would you most like to go on at the fair?"

Use the story trail to encourage your child to retell the story in the right sequence, in their own words.

Extending learning

Help your child understand the story structure by using the same sentence patterns and adding some new elements. "Let's make up a new story about Jack and Mish going to the fair. In my story they are on going on a bouncy castle. Mum says: 'Don't bounce too high!' But Jack doesn't listen and bounces as high as he can and falls off. Now you try. What will they go on in your story?"

Your child's teacher will be talking about punctuation at Yellow Band. On a few of the pages, check your child can recognise capital letters, full stops, exclamation marks and speech marks by asking them to point these out.

Franklin Watts
First published in Great Britain in 2017
by The Watts Publishing Group

Copyright © The Watts Publishing Group 2017

Series Editors: Jackie Hamley and Melanie Palmer
Series Advisors: Dr Sue Bodman and Glen Franklin
Series Designer: Peter Scoulding

A CIP catalogue record for this book is
available from the British Library.

ISBN 978 1 4451 5469 5 (hbk)
ISBN 978 1 4451 5470 1 (pbk)
ISBN 978 1 4451 6079 5 (library ebook)

Printed in China

Franklin Watts
An imprint of
Hachette Children's Group
Part of The Watts Publishing Group
Carmelite House
50 Victoria Embankment
London EC4Y 0DZ

An Hachette UK Company
www.hachette.co.uk

www.franklinwatts.co.uk